AfterW

Pauline Dr

£1.00

To aria

enjoy

1 ove

Pauline

14/12/09

Acknowledgement to Conroy Maddox for the cover illustration

Published November 2008 by Lilyville Press

ISBN 978-0-9548882-8-2

Printed in Great Britain by
**Lonsdale Press Ltd, 43-47 Lonsdale Road,
Queen's Park, London NW6 6RA**

I dedicate this book to
Caroline and Christopher in California

Contents

AfterWords

After words what comes - a gesture, a nod, a smile,
a change of mood or feeling?
Words, words, words, so marvellous, so important,
so deceiving, so rhetorical - and so often
inadequate.
But that's all we have -
Choose them with care.

Transient

We laughed together
on sandy beaches.
Danced into the sea
drifting into hot noons.

We drank wine in the sun,
drowsing through siesta
love locked in our arms
as ripening fruit fell.

And at night hot winds
blew stars across the sky
as we drew lots
for the one who could love longest.

Early Morning Scene

Voices of the morning
          come on the wind
sharp dog barks, complaining cows
          the low buzz of insects.

Across the dampened fields
          blackbirds
like musical notation
          line telegraph wires.

Leaving the rhythms of a rural scene
the early train carries workers to the
stir and clamour of a northern town.

Along the canal
          a solitary fisher
looks at the sky, shrugs off rain.

Watching The Day

I have been watching the day
Hour by hour,
Light changing all the time
Sun, wind, clouds never the same
All moving inexorably on.

Early morning fresh, full of hope
Birds loud, light dazzling,
Creatures taking each moment as it comes.

It's the small things that are part of the day:
The rustle of leaves as the wind passes
The clouds lowering over the sun
The bird on a tree -
The enchantment of a thousand daffodils
Nodding their yellow crowns in early spring.

Watching the day moment to moment
Casts a spell that could be called happiness.

Flyer Hawk

And then I saw the Hawk
its hard flapping wings
keeping guard over one space
and the quick glitter of eye
watching, waiting, tense
in high concentration.

And then the swift dart down
to a high pitched scream
of some captured creature
now beak enclosed and
pitched in flight.

And then the powered flight
disappearing from blue into green.

Winter

Winter's cold and dark
only love gives warmth and light
two fires burn snow-banked.

Views On A Crow

1. First Light
   crow grabs breakfast
   worms soft: strawberries sweet.

2. Air-less noon - no wind breathes
   stark, black crow
   carrion lunch.

3. Sun scorches afternoon
   time sleeps
   crow flies.

4. Sun slips paling sky
   crows in flocks
   gathering.

5. Dusk mantles tree tops
   beckons the evening star
   crow saunters for grain.

6. Stars like silver milk tops
   lighten darkness
   crow wings into night.

7. Milk tops like stars
   gleam on dawn's doorstep
   crow plunders.

Cows Drink And Graze

June sunlight flickers through
                    old oaks
as slowly they walk down
                    to drink
For the River beckons.
Lowered heads dip in dignified
                    silence
long tongues drinking down
                    water.
Refreshed, together they turn
and plod upbank to graze again.
A lush meadow fortifies the
                    black and white.
These sturdy and so-useful
                    creatures
Move in peaceful unison
Unaware of market's future
                    slaughter.

Summer Landscape

The tawny grass
Catches the August wind;
ripening gold speckled with red
dances close to the night air
before gentle rain waters the
                ripening plains.
Now the fullness of the moon
adds silver to gold
while night creatures awake to
foraging in bright shadows.
June's greenest green now
coloured to high summer
awaits the gathering harvest and
I lie in ecstasy under the
                darkening sky.

Brondesbury 4 p.m.

The flowers are cold
autumn frost has nipped their vigour.
Station platforms glisten
from melted fog as children,
freed from school, climb their homeward train.
Along the tracks
grass glitters silver-green
and unfurled petals look uncertain
under winter sun.

Journey Back

The tree-teased sun kaleidoscopes
past images of summer
As I delight in November's frosty
stillness.

Along the canal birds silver the water
dipping for fish.
The long boats stand empty now
summerless
Their bright colours muted by
autumn's light.

Beyond the banks an isolated church
stands sentinel
Beside a water meadow that feeds
grazing cattle
Their rural peace now so fragile.
I journey on to another reality.

The Wind

Then the Wind came up
North by north-west
Howling, growling, snarling
It bent the trees and broke the weak
Its force battering power lines
And the sound of falling, breaking and
Smashing glass went on and on
Back and forth all night long.
People died along its course.
It drove grassland into knife-like waves
In a kind of beauty and
Jolted birds in its mighty breath,
Frantic wings trying to keep their line.
Clouds turned around as it ravaged rooftops
Scattering garden fences like dice.
Seaside waves breached all defences
Crashing and drowning upstreet houses
Going places it had never been before.

Nothing could stand against its rage
When the wind came by - north by north-west that day.

Fog

Fog is like a cold, wet kiss
Like arms embracing air
Like eyes unsure of seeing
Like misted glass distorting
Like spectacles steamed up.

Fog makes everything look
Different, romantic, eerie, mysterious,
Evoking daydreams, nightmares -
        imaging mysteries
It is reality but somehow unreal.

Winter Dawn

Water stretching before me
into darkness,
and out there the geese
are waiting.
Suddenly it's first light -
a rush of wings
Flying victory shaped.
Then more and more
With a roar of wild high cries
and beating wings
Glorious Pinkfoots fly fro mThe Wash
crowding to feed.
Spread like great arrowheads
They curve into dawn
Heading for the beet fields
criss-crossing over
The long dark line - leaving water
They come in to land.

14

Winterscape

Only the crows startle
On dull brown fields
Their cries strung out
        on winter air.

Bare hills gently recede
Onto long laid furrows
Where sods lie in a
Mute and misty land.

At my road's edge a line
Of elegant poplars stand
Sentinels to past plantation.
My day is dusk all through.

A water rail, startled,
Flash-flies in feathered rust
Over the pruned coppice
Before crossing the rushing stream.

I stand contemplating land
That represents another England
Rural, isolate, at peace,
Much the same as Domesday charted -
Precious, dying, hidden
        Winterscape.

Winter Seas

I like watching
alone in the blustered cold
where gulls mew along the wind
the sea all mine in its metallic foreboding.

The rhythms of its ancient ebb and flow
succour my hibernating mind
quietening the senses by its heaving bleakness.

Often those Summer days of blue-mist heat
all hectic and expectant, disappoint;
their morning's arousal lapsed by evening
into sensual lethargy.

Now, the seaside town devoid of colour
is etched in mezzotint
dreaming itself into peaceful Christmastide.

Sometimes drama is enacted as storms
hurl waves over man-made barriers -
challenging promenade tea-rooms with flood.

I watch fearfully, justly in awe
as the pounding waters rise unrestrained
their fierce magnificence wreaking revenge
on thoughts of Summer's sandcastles.

Their thunder dominates the night as I lie
restless, my body, my heartbeat cradled
by primeval rhythms
acknowledging aeons of water kinship.

Winter's Edge

Snow falls like tears
From hedges and trees
A deep melting into winter's edge.

The cloud so low and white
It nearly meets the road
And birds black and cold
Fly in between.

Then the silence -
People gliding quickly home
Afraid to slip, afraid to stop -
Living in another consciousness
In an all-changed landscape
Making the ordinary
Extraordinary.

Such stark beauty
Breathing its icy breath
Into our regular lives.

Elephant In A landscape

Ears flap
        heat dense
                ancient grey
                        silhouette in dust

Crane

Red crowned crane stirs
Stalking along river's edge
Beauty catches fish.

Frost

When the frost lies white
Whooper swans split winter air
Drama in beauty.

Three Haiku

There is a moment
When the magnolia blossoms
Perfect in beauty

Loneliness of sky
Reflects forgotten water
There, birds are silent

The world is yellow
As spring arrives with hope
Glory in rain and sun.

For The Dead

The Pharoahs took the loot
    To heaven with them

Their tombs filled with goodies
    Afterlife assured.

Memorials were hidden deep
    Secret and safe

Their outer world became reflected
    in the hereafter

Later ages made marble or stone
    Their memorial
Everything grand for bereaved feelings
    Along cemetery rows
They had access with words and flowers
    Memories made concrete in stone.

Ritual, dignity, craftsmanship gave meaning
    To the dead.

But now a short obit:
    a swift goodbye
Before that tramlined move to fire
Is all we get when we expire.

An Imaginary Ending To Giorgio De Chirico's
"*Mystery And Melancholy Of The Street*" - 1914

Feeling along the edges of a shadowed street
I seek to know where it leads
what it could reveal.
Is the shadowed spectre one of sadness
or merely the heavy shade of some long forgotten fame?
A door awaits, open as are all the doors, their shadows
lengthening into the deadening noon-time heat
shedding a sinister mood to a simple scene.

A child plays alone. Will she enter into
caverns of mystery and delight or
is her innocence threatened?
If two shadows meet and mingle
what awful coupling may take place and then
the mystery and melancholy of the street
might regard with half-shut eyes
death in the afternoon?

Outward and onward I go not knowing where or why
into some covered dreamland where by chance
some strange encounter may greet my wandering soul
There, one could be thankful for a chance to learn
what reality exists beyond art, beyond time,
Is it a reality that trembles like a promise of hope
or terror?
Or is it my life that awaits at the end of the street?

Travelling Time

What am I doing here
        I ask myself?
Travelling alone again
Musing in Ireland's Springtime.

Unattached observer recording
        time and space
In another country, empathising
Through a past of valedictions.

The surface appears unruffled, calm.
The world of friendly voices welcoming;
But beneath, history's forces show
Fragments of a culture ridden hard by time.

Unbelievable calumnies mark this land
In memory - History contrasts
With genial faces, jokes in the pub
Local gossip connecting communities.

But I seek that which is left
Feeling on the pulse of things
An ancient echo where something remains
Undefeated: an essence that connects
        Myth to fact.

No divisions mark out this territory -
The beauty of the landscape remains.
Here waters flow clean and clear
Endless rain washing down sky to land
Where the feckless plover yields to sand.

I am here in memories, listening to loving
Voices calling across a lonely Strand.

In Connemara

In Connemara layers of rock
 Echo time's age
Names have changed but not space
Nor the lingering light over
 Islands of water.
Here survivors can be beached,
 Washed up, stranded
On rocks, monolithic: the silence
 Buffeted on wind.
The sea out there waits empty
 Surging unobserved.
Inland they've heard of one who
 Sought a watery grave.

The Past Is With Us Still

Always in anger and hate we warred.
Stern myths primed us on
 Into darker labyrinths.
Tales and lies, lies and tales.

Our history tells of calumnies
Against ill defined borders -
Of shifting landmarks
 Recording violence and death.
Tales and lies, lies and tales.

We made war a habit that bled hearts.
Oh pale antagonist
When the rat in the skull
Gnaws at your soul take care
 For surely you know
 For whom the die is cast.
Tales and lies, lies and tales.

Armistice Day 2007

They have gone and we are left
In a world fast fading.
They fought for freedom
For a better world for children
To play, to learn, to love.

Now, we have to fight for survival
Against the forces of a dying nature
Carelessly stirred into deadly action.

Are we sorry now for
Becoming the ultimate enemy?

Bitter Harvest

That year the harvest was good.
Golden wheat flowing among poppy red
    Birds gleaning free
Men had reaped hard and were content.

    Then all changed.

Fields became dark mounds of mud
    Blood was the red
As men harvested men in death
Boys lived like rats - youth in despair.

Big Guns - echoing blasts, falling shells,
A sky crossed by lightning fire
Exploding - men illuminated as they
Broke apart out of the earth holes of their lives.

Sometimes a dangerous silence brought birdsong -
Then suddenly, like a writhing snake,
A pool of luminous green engendered
A shuddering, a gasping, a contortion
in the final indignity of dying.

Soldiers

We went not quite knowing
what to expect -
what to expect from ourselves.
We knew all about guns, bombs, death
               in theory.
But we went thinking -
it won't happen to us, to me
things will be ok.
After all it's a job, we chose it,
we trained for it.
Everything would be alright.

But of course it wasn't -
our world was turned upside down.
Nothing happened as it should,
there was death alright and
wounding, pain and torture and
the endless killing. But
it didn't happen to other people.
It happened to us, to me.

And we can never be the same again.
If we return we'll never be able to say:
You understand
Because you never will, never can,
and our words can never describe
what occurred there,
and what happened to us, to me,
inside.

We are exiles caught
in the timewarp of War.

A Journey

Strangers travelling together,
I liked his face - expressive
How easy it would have been
To have loved him.

The train eating up the suburbs
Moving into light and space,
How good it would have been
To have talked to him.

His perfect, private Englishness
Mystified, attracted me
How lovely it would have been
To have held his hand.

Stations flashed past - No stops
Until, halt: he alighted - I sat on.
How nice it would have been
To have got off together.

Lovely Las Vegas

Neon lit city
Rising out of the desert
In a blaze of colour.

Vegas, the brash place
Middle of nowhere town
Where dawn and sunset meet.

The sound of sax and trumpet
Echo the chink of chips
Coke and hamburger land.

Tall showgirls kick high
While crooners lilt to shuffling cards.
Too many cigarette ends

Bourbon and black coffee consolations
For stakes that jump too high.
Lovely one-armed bandits.

High bosomed blondes drift through
Quick divorces, brief encounters.
Hangovers linger over green tables.

Vegas, Queen of the Desert
Lighted out of her mind
Hit and run town - Shambles.

No Questioner

I sit upon the precarious
curve of a question mark but
I do not know any answers
to any questions that I may pose.

Someone, sometime said
don't waste your time young man
there are no answers anyway
life's a sham, just live it out
to pleasure's plan and let it be.

So still I sit upon that
curve and watch the world go by
and I don't care to understand
what comes to pass
no questioner am I.

Forgiveness

Understanding is a kind of
        Forgiving
It liberates the heart when love
        Has been betrayed,
The anger, the hurt, the bitterness
        Dies at last
        In forgiveness

Perfect?

Why is it called the perfect Tense?
I don't see anything perfect about it.
        Perfect is now -
        The present tense.

Dry Dock

The landscape of my mind is coloured black and grey
my map's expanse is watered by deep untroubled sea
and yet I do not know myself, except perhaps to say
I'm landlocked by a dark lagoon and cannot break away.

There is no boat in which to sail through stormy waves
to seek and find those coloured shores that I myself deny.
My will lies in stasis my little courage misbehaves
and nothing seems to change me and no-one comes to save.

My life's made up of nothing, a life that seems unreal
lived at others beck and call, sharing their regrets.
I wish that you could stab me or tread me under-heel
that blood would flow and anger let me really feel.

I come and go in regular routine, boredom strikes my clock
and seasons pass without event or love's sharpened blows;
Against the window I turn my back, the room I merely mock
but who am I and where am I? - on trial in my dry-dock.

The Panthers

Sometimes at night the panthers come
Their feline blackness out to destroy
I am their prey heart and soul the sum
of parts with which they make ploy.

Within dark, secret places they savage me
blackness descending into confusion
their green-glint eyes pierce and ravage me
I fall to rotating wheels of delusion.

Entangled in their underworld - I cry
as their teeth tear, twist me down,
down and down it's the old lie
this devil's game and I play pawn
cannot jump or move to rightful place.
They, in merciless power make leap
I am lost - gone without trace
a dark oblivion my prison keep.

When struggling blackness gives way
Exhausted I surface, grasp dim light of day.

A Change Of Life

A change of life is like
Learning a new language
Jumbled words, incoherence
Then suddenly a complete sentence
And we enter a new life.

Being is doing in essence
Being is having in everything

We need not hurt one another
Or be in pain alone
If the heart is right my brother
Recognize we are on loan.

Taking Tea

She sat in subdued elegance
Alone, sad, slightly prim.
An end to romantic love perhaps
Had left traces around her eyes.
Or was it loss of another kind?

I pondered on and catching sighs
I wrote 'obituary' to her gaze
over tea-cups, cakes and scones.
My diagnosis over I glanced at another
dreaming afternoon's last hour away.

There's melancholy innate in solo tea
And mine was also one of these
Perhaps it was after all my own state
That saw their's reflected in the plate.

Now You Are Gone

Now you are gone
emptiness - unbearable
icy winds freeze my heart

now you are gone
I'm left with all the negatives
of those images we saw together
in the burnt out camera of time

now you are gone
I hold fast to the bars
of my little prison

now you are gone
picking up the pieces
is more difficult
than mending shattered glass.

As I Look Across

As I look across
The darkening sea at dusk
Loneliness lingers
Remembering you, tears fall,
Past happiness brings sadness.

Standing here alone
I remember our days together.
Tears fall silently
I wish the past would return
For just one more hour with you.

Betrayed

You are betrayed:
the world was an oyster
which gave no pearl.

Spiked by the savage spear
you lost the irredeemable -
now are inconsolable.

As the fox steals by stealth
so all creatures are part fox.

Paranoia

She heard them mutter again
Her head buzzed with
vicious wires of gossip,
animus wore her to the bone.
The doctor nodded, vacuous, hardly patient
as she related endless enmities
that hemmed in her day.
The barbed territories of her existence
constantly threatened when
in the open street all gestures menaced
causing her breath to shallow
her heart to faint and fall.
As she passed her garden gate
neighbours turned, smiling secretly.
Her mind, distorting, misprinting
all messages, called
the world a hostile place.

"Goodbye"

It is the hour of departure.
Like white handkerchiefs
the clouds travel on the wind
saying goodbye to summer dreams;
and you, you stand on the quay
a ship to the unknown.
Because the resonance of my dreams
cannot compare to past reality
I cut from the slipways of my mind all memory -
like a disappearing wake all traces vanish.
I stand, free.

Later, leaning into the dusk
the bright beam of the lighthouse
penetrates - there is no freedom -
the shackles, like rocks are always there.
Love is short, forgetting so long.

Departure

You silently slipped away
And I unaware
Until the soft dawn air
Alerted me.
For there you lay
Your face all peace - but I
All rage of grief asked why
Why it was you - not me?

Woman In Winter

I am a woman in winter,
all griefs sealed in
all fires dampened down
and the shafts going nowhere.

I am a woman in extremis
still alive but waiting to die
holding threads so thin
that no light can hold them.

Once there was a summer
half remembered in a blaze of time
a time that only teased the brain
and made memory lie.

I am a woman in winter
and the cold covers my land
now with a surge of ice
the hands of time must close.

Accident

Sudden braking, noise exploding,
     Pain splinters me.
     I am cracked glass
Tasting salt in the blood.

Then falling, falling into petrified air.
     Sirens score the street
As quickly, quickly they almost
     Tenderly lift me, hold me;
     I am still alive.

On The Edge

We live on the edge -
of life, of others, of ourselves,
Trapped on the other side of the wind
halfway in, halfway out.
Memories wind around us
making the present, the past
until perhaps the looking back is all we've got -
all that's left - a long vista of sunsets
before our own.

Love's Gone

Your bed's a grave
And I lie tossed and
Turned the long night
Adrift from your presence,
Memories not enough
      To hide in.

I overspend my days
And in the evenings
Love turns to pain
The syntax having
Lost its way again.

I cannot look outward,
Am still contained in you
Although part of me knows
Soon I should seek
For someone new.

I live my face disguised
My feelings barriered behind
      A hidden glass.
Somewhere a voice echoes
Like a bird's call calling
Take off your disguise
And dispel the past.

Lost Autumn

I remember September and the farmers finishing up.
All harvest over - there was a dying down into
      A long October
Then the berries were picked, jams and pickles made
And we ate liberally, all content.
I, a child, couldn't reach the table
And had to climb my brother's knee
To rest my arms and eat.
Memories remain of play and work and sunlit hours
Before it turned to dust as the season's
Grain diseased and dead forced us
To leave and start all over again.

I well remember
My father's voice all tired and harsh as
My mother wept.
Travelling north I saw
The tips of the hills sun-setted and beautiful
As we drove the weary miles into winter
Never to know such secure happiness again.

Now I am grown into an urban man
Discontent and tired, unable to see
Autumn's glory in the same way
      Ever again.

A Pocket Picked

Don't stick your hands in your pockets
Mum always said,
Why?
Because it ruins their shape.
Oh!
But
I liked keeping my hands warm
jingling my coins for sweets
maybe stopping pickpockets.

But now I am old
I forgot all about it.

I had my pension stolen today
Just because
I didn't have my hands
in my pockets.

Inside Out

Sometimes my body feels as if
    it's inside out
Like an old sweater with seams exposed
    Revealing imperfections.
"It's bad luck to take off an
inside-out jumper" Mum had said.
And that's how I felt.
    As a child I always wore
Inside-out vests
Revelling in that rebellious act.
"You'll grow up all wrong" Mum had said.
She was right of course.
But I still like that furtive feel
Of the right-side against my skin.
A secret, sensuous feeling -
An act of rebellion
Against the outside world.